CATCHING SUNDOWN

CATCHING SUNDOWN

Poems

Peter C. Leverich

Peter C. Leverich

Copyright © 2006 by Peter C. Leverich.

ISBN 10:	Hardcover	1-4257-2772-7
	Softcover	1-4257-2771-9
ISBN 13:	Hardcover	978-1-4257-2772-7
	Softcover	978-1-4257-2771-0

All rights reserved. No part of this book may be reproduced or transmitted in any form or by any means, electronic or mechanical, including photocopying, recording, or by any information storage and retrieval system, without permission in writing from the copyright owner.

This book was printed in the United States of America.

To order additional copies of this book, contact:
Xlibris Corporation
1-888-795-4274
www.Xlibris.com
Orders@Xlibris.com
35851

for Diane
my North Star

Curious indeed that in this life, brief and precariously enjoyed, men should so set their hearts on building a permanence in words: something to stand, in the lovely stability of ink and leaden types, as our speech out of silence to those who follow on. Indefensible absurdity, and yet the secret and impassioned dream of those who write.

          Christopher Morley

CONTENTS

1. Treble Clef
2. Morning Song
3. Diamond Alley
4. Nassau Point
5. Land's End
6. Terns
7. Bay View
9. Tidewaters
10. Before Morning
11. Peconic Still
12. I Never Pray for Bass
14. By the Light of the Silvery Moon
16. Longevity
17. Clams on the Half Shell
18. Night Rain
19. Country Roads
20. Spring Birch
21. Garden Girls
22. Poppies
23. Main Street
24. The Fourth of July
25. Grandfather was a Dapper Man
26. The Vines
27. Southold Chardonnay
28. Elegy for Aunt Ella
29. Osprey Sky High
31. Impresarios

32. Sprite
33. Prelude
34. Polaris
35. Oracle
36. Charade
37. Quintet for Terns
38. Shooting Stars
39. Sandpipers
40. Soft
41. $E=mc^2$
42. Archimedes Principle
43. Doxology
44. Geonyms
45. Caprice
46. Floating
47. Still Light
48. Windfall
49. A Sunset Sail with You
50. Cartography
51. Vow at Summer's End
52. Swingtime
53. Now They Grow Roses
54. Speaking of Fish
55. A Week on the Bay
56. Fisherman's Beach
57. Divine Rites
58. North Fork Fall
59. Reflection
60. Equinox
61. Rose's Grove
62. Perfection
64. Catching Sundown

65. Snowbound
66. Leit Motif
67. SnowFly
68. Duck Tips
69. Cloud Nine
70. Orient Blue
72. Dwelling in Cedars
74. Tacking Towards Home

77. Acknowledgements
79. About the Author

*You ask me why I live by the bay.
I smile at such a question –*

as ebb and flow
wind water and light
a stunning quartet
in a natural key
is playing *con brio*
right here
right where you're standing.

inspired by Li Bai 李白

Morning Song

The morning bay
flicks at the beach
with sanded tongues
like a thousand cats
testing their milk.

A white rustle
at the water's hem
and the gawk of gulls
at the tip of the point
are the only sounds.

At my approach
a tawny hare
rabbits to safety
from under the dock.

I start at such quickness
before breakfast.

Diamond Alley

The A-frame is set
as close to the bay
as zoning allows.
When the sun is out
visibility at its best
the southwest vista
unfurls for miles on end.

The slightest stir of air
riffles the surface;
under shell-blue skies
banks of cumulus clouds
the architecture of fantasy
tower over the ridge
that outlines the South Fork.

As far as the eye can see
small puddles of sunshine
stipple the bay.
A river of diamonds
sweeps past Nassau Point
between Robins Island
the great bluff at Southampton

all the way to Shinnecock.

Nassau Point

These lands belong to the privileged
to the achievers the inheritors and to the lucky dealers
those who having wrested more than other men
from the struggles of commerce and of living
take refuge here winding out their days
in quietness and in small grandeur.
Through their good fortune the call of the jay
still rings in the leaves of the locust trees,
through their good fortune roses in red profusion
still tumble to the beach down the western slope.

Land's End

The point beyond the point
that graceful ess
of sand of stone of shell
that sweeps into the bay
for almost one mile
to the red channel bell
warning boatmen off the shoal
is no man's land.

Not even the gulls
that squat there
half submerged
can hold their perch
when wind and opposing tide
drive the bay from east and west
in sheets of sizzling white
across the bar like butter
dancing on a hot spit.

Terns

Quicksilver
a glint of tern
flash of arched wing
then sky in a downpour
of sun burnished birds
bursting from blue over the bay
thirty yards off shore
down the beach from my house.

The bay is teeming with bait
a bumper crop of silver clad spearing
clustered in schools;
wilding bluefish drive them to light,
they leap for the sky
in a frantic attempt to escape extinction,
the higher they leap the easier it is
for stiletto beaked birds to take them in air.

Marauding blues
now in front of my deck
churn bay water white
the sky is a torrent
of fish frenzied terns
it is late afternoon one Sunday in July
cottagers come forward to witness the fray
a silent ovation wide eyed and struck.

Bay View

The bay does not intimidate
like the mountain
It uses influence
throws its weight around
shakes hands
slaps backs
kisses babies
shows up for barbecues

The bay is user friendly
unlike the sound
with its too steep bluffs
bouldered shoreline
rocky beaches
rough waves
and winter winds that blow
the shingles off a barn

The bay is reflective
pink at dawn gold by day
red at sundown
white by night
its splashing shades
color the clouds
bounce light off the bluffs
and the window panes

The bay keeps moving
day and night
the tide floods the tide ebbs
winds embroider
pleat and tuck
fish flip clams spit
stones skip
it never rests

The bay provides
flounder filets
chowder and bisque
crab cake supreme
scallop flambé
but better than food
the bay provides perspective too
its moment changes every scale.

Tidewaters

That boulder which lay midway on the beach
the same one my two year old climbed
in wobbly triumph only last weekend
is gone from sight today
covered now by sands
which soon will fill the summer beach.

I recollect another beach at another time
a man and a boy digging the sand
as if the ebb and flow did not pertain.
The man is gone now on the outward tide,
the boy has moved inland
and for a while
my son and I build castles here.

Before Morning

Sun up
a vane of brightness
a bleed
a bloom
an aura of white
unsung and unseen
while the North Fork sleeps
a burst of rayed light
above Paradise Point
sky tinged pink
peach painted clouds
a quiet crescendo
bright brass
big red drum

Peconic Still

The bay is hushed today
nobody knows it's here
not even the absent wind
who has left a cat's paw scrim
like fingerprints on glass.

I Never Pray for Bass

I think you'd agree
the good Lord has better things to do
than worry about setting a hook
in the bony mouth
of a prize winning line-sider,
but my nephew Jeff
had come a long way to wet a line.

When we reached Plum Gut
and found that place we call the *G Spot,*
because it's ninety feet deep
and the current runs strong there,
I shut my eyes hard
then under my breath
Lord, this boy has traveled for bass,
now don't let me down.

We fished for an hour,
the tide was running,
white bucktails streamed
behind heavy lead sinkers.
Then I felt it,
a power in the water,
an unmistakable vibrancy,
like a séance when the spirit
has entered the room,
that's when Jeff said
I've got one on.

When we finally saw it,
ten feet from the boat,
a thrashing rainbow
of burgundy and silver,
a strapping striper
with a menacing dorsal fin
slashing the surface,
it seemed almost too large.

But in a splurge of white water,
it wound up in our net —
forty two inches long
and twenty three pounds.
I was happy that Jeff caught his fish,
it was one inch short and two pounds light
of the family record
a bass I landed single-handedly,
only last year.

By the Light of the Silvery Moon

Go
light
moon

show
the argent
bay

how silver
night
can be.

Oh
bright
moon

silver
on your
strings

strike
a light
arpeggio.

Lo
white
moon

stun
the morning
sky

wafer
thin and
sterling.

Longevity

At the end of May
when the moon is full
just after the sun has set
horseshoe crabs crawl in from the deep
and nest in the sands
around Broadwaters Cove.

Cows and bulls
with barnacled backs
spawn in groups of two and three,
there is some perverseness in nature too.
The waterline is a collar of foam
with churning creatures partly washed
by lulling wave and flooding tide.

The evening is still
but there is this awesome stir
of a species prolonging its race.
Fossils prove they have existed
for more than a million years —
older even than dinosaurs.
Yet I know that in a few weeks
I will find the tiny transparent shells
of their unsuccessful offspring
wantonly strewn along the beach.

Clams on the Half Shell

    Gull
          after
                gull
                      after
                            gull

feathery *corps de ballet*
gliding in place
a backdrop of blue
riding the winds
at the edge of the bay
where breaking waves
toss shellfish on sand

scavenging gulls
SWOOOP in for the catch
quahogs and conchs
carried high in the sky
dropped on the rocks
to crack o p e n their shells.

Night Rain

Unseasonable
all this rain in June,
just three days dry
in three wet weeks,
but weather has its way.
The sky tonight
is draped with clouds
swart and shadowed crepe
in scalloped swags
backlit by an obscured moon
row upon row
above the inkberry bay.
In the great room looking out
awash with this dark scape
I am as whole as the rain.

Country Roads

I live in town
but there are no down-town sounds
no car alarms
no traffic noise
no sirens
a quiet soul evokes its own seclusion.

I wander down a dusty country road
amidst a rustling sea of cool green corn
the road is perfectly straight
with telephone poles precisely aligned
on either side as far as one can see.
As my musing drifts out east
I am deeply moved
but fumble for the words that tell.

Spring Birch

Only Renoir
could paint such a tree
a burly birch with a triple trunk
bursting to white
from a blackened base
in its branches
a continent of green leaves
tremble before the blue eye
of a clear God.

Garden Girls

Raucous geraniums
redder than lipstick
banal and brazen
lacking finesse
like factory girls —

broad leafed
stocky stemmed
thick headed bloomers
shocking the summer
with such easy virtue.

Poppies

Silken cuplets
detonate June
in a tumult
of short lived color.

Randy progenitors
prodigal spillers of pollen
lavishly propagate
their windborne palette
of bright eyed beauty.

Main Street

s k y

wide empty space

motes of dust
trapped in shafts of Attic light

serenity simplicity order
sunshine and shadow
structures of primary color

notes of a chiming hymn
afloat from the Methodist Church

a red pickup truck
waiting for the light

12 o'clock noon
Southold.

The Fourth of July

My friends go to France
I stay home
I don't hate the French
I love America. My forefather,
long before Washington's,
came to these shores.
He was a Whig and a Puritan
a graduate of Cambridge.
I don't think there is a statute
of limitations on liberty.

Liberty in 1776
if you were not native American
a woman or a slave
meant you were free to pursue.
Adams willed it
Washington won it
Jefferson wrote it
the Engine the Sword and the Pen.
Who hasn't heard of the liberty gene
I am struck with it
what about you ?

Grandfather was a Dapper Man

even his children were nicely dressed and posed
whenever they were in the company of their father.
He smoked a pipe and looked like a proper gentleman
his name was William.

Three piece suit
                fedora hat
                              wing-tip shoes

his two oldest boys
                in blazers and rep ties
                straw boaters with tricolor bands

his baby son
                in white piqu'e

nicely arranged
        top to bottom
                on the front porch steps

as if sitting for a portrait
        that would surely be admired
                down a litany of generations.

The Vines

Farmers are vintners now
cauliflower and corn gone to grapes
potato fields to vinyards
each one vaunting its grower's pride
chardonnay merlot pinot noir blanc de blanc
each a tidy regiment
leafy green vines on wooden legs
a verdant militia aligned in neat rows.

Wine is an attraction
on weekends people come
to stand and sip in tasting rooms.
They buy sunflowers tee shirts and cork-screws.
The North Fork unrequited all these years
is courted now; old timers carp
too much sprawl too many cars
but the landscape makes you gasp
green glossy lush and yes
gentrified.

Southold Chardonnay

The warmth of the sun
trapped on a sunlit afternoon
clusters of swollen grapes
barely constrained in rows
bursting with juice
straw yellow and clear.

One sip rolls up in a ball
butter on your tongue
a season of growing green
extracted in a single drop
a hint of oak on the palate
bouquet by Van Gogh
vin de fleur du soleil!

Elegy for Aunt Ella

One by one

into
      God's
           garden
                  they go

rowdy boys
salty girls
reluctant transplants

leather-lunged lads
bright-tongued beauties

hybrids more rare
than any white marigold.

Osprey Sky High

hinged-wing glider
scours in decorous
sharp eyed gyres
divines sans shadow
schools of scaled scup
darting at depths
murky to plumb

a gathering up
wings furled close
streamlined to plunge
briefly freeze framed
sudden cant bayward
compulsion to dive
in mindless descent
lustful of fish

spray white spume
opalescence of spearing
seized in talons
a fathom below
ruckus of wing beat
commotion of brine
wings spanned wide
racking thin air

weighty path aerborne
struggling with prey
dragged from the tide
upwards to blue
reflection of sunlight
glitter of scales
skims the steep bluff
fading from view.

Impresarios

Low tide exposes a flat
mud and sand pocked by burrows
each one home to a fiddler crab.
Frantically bowing
with one jumbo claw
the male tries to entice a mate
in hopes that tempo and melody
will preserve his place
in the gene pool of maestros.
When the flood tide turns
these littoral virtuosos
choosing safety instead of applause
disappear down their burrows
where they wait *pianissimo*
for the next ebbing tide.

Sprite

Acrobat with ruby throat
defying death in a lucentious whirrr
like a Flying Wallenda
high above the gasping daffodils.
Feathery Casanova
tonguing each trumpet
on the trellis vine
entering the orifice
of each columbine
unaware the tremolo in your breast
is part of the role you play
to leave no blossom chaste.

Prelude

Twilight beguiles the gazer
who weaves it into dreams
as the heat of the day transforms itself
like passion's softened afterglow.
The sunset's melted pastel sky
is prelude to this interval
impending darkness hesitates
then shows the evening star
before embracing satin night.

Polaris

As universe expands
star by star will dim
until some day men see
blackness in the firmament.

The last celestial fires

    sun's brightness reflected
    by moons planets and asteroids

    a trail of atomic light
    as shooting stars fly past

    bursts of fire as meteors
    incinerate in atmosphere

With so much starlight lost

    comets more visible then
    will swim their lazy course
    across the cosmic sea.

But stars are bright this night
lustrous milky way
Polaris is still in its place
five times distant
on a straight line
above the Big Dipper's cup.

Oracle

A giant heron makes her home
in the tallest trees around Brick Cove.

A great slate blue bird
she wades in the shallows
on stilt like legs,
her neck a graceful feathery ess.
She can be still for so long
that she seems in a trance
but finally takes a practiced step
without causing a ripple
as she stalks fish for food.

Because of her size
she is left alone,
if you come too close
she will burst into flight
and leave you in awe
without even one answer.

Charade

Meditation has no end
as I watch the lighthouse
on Little Gull Island
silhouetted by the setting sun.

Evening waters are still
flowers of sunlight
slowly adrift
encircle my boat.

I choose this evening in August
to cloak myself in serenity
and to be just a man
fishing for bass.

Quintet for Terns

Silver dollar terns
kite and cut cross and die
in kamikaze dives
reborn in salty spray
free verse
flashing words wild syllables
unpredictable at best
but always in a form
imposed by flight's free way
to nature's highest power.

Shooting Stars

The moon in the western sky
is bent like an archer's bow.

In front of the graceful arc
the evening star is poised
a glowing arrowhead
ready to be raised aimed
pulled taut against the string
and fired with just a *pfssst*

at the first fiery glimpse
of any shooting star.

Sandpipers

Towheads
trailing plastic pails
criss-cross beach and time
in stitches of energy
small bursts of wonder.

Wide eyed
hair blown
salt skinned
Sam and Chris and Shelley
discovering in the wrack

slipper shells jingle shells
and best of all a craggy old crab shell
with protruding eyes still intact
which being real
overawes every creature on TV.

Soft

Weather is soft today
there's roundness in the air
a dewy dilution of crispness
sky Caribbean blue
cresting with cumulus waves
a cloud-surfer's summer come true.

Weather is sheer today
there's subtlety in the light
a burnished blurring of edges
the point across the bay
cast shadowy in relief
beyond that deepening mist.

Weather is sluggish today
there's solace in the warmth
the balm of tempered sun
scented wind rumples the bay
muted and dulcet
like rose petals fallen.

E=mc²

Einstein summered on Nassau Point.
He described the Peconic Bay
the most beautiful sailing grounds
I ever experienced.
His boat was named *Tineff*
a Yiddish word that means worthless.
Since he couldn't swim
he had no business out on a boat
but sailing gave him time to think
to reduce to one formula the explanation
of the field of gravity and . . . electromagnetism.

He kept to himself most of the time
but some evenings played the violin.
After Brahms on the screened in porch
he spoke about planets that orbit the sun
electrons that orbit the nucleus of an atom
I'm not so much interested in the particles
he said *as the spaces between them.*
By choosing to summer on Nassau Point
and sailing for hours on the Peconic Bay
he proved himself
                               a man of true genius.

Archimedes Principle

While God and mother looked away
her brown body
slid between the glittery blue water
and as silently as a shadow
slipped to the bottom of the pool
where in four feet of depth
two more than her years
she drowned unobserved
in a commotion of ripples
and a spate of rushing bubbles.

Three days later
on a sunlit summer morning
she was buried in St. Patrick's Cemetery.
Mourners did not question gravity
or the other principles of physical law
as they heard again about The Resurrection
and in spite of the heat that week
nobody swam in the pool.

Doxology

Church music
from a kitchen radio
across sunlit yards
fragrant with lilacs

Organ and choir
resonant with remembrance
of early childhood mornings
in warm rooms with eaves
over a celebration of Sundays

Geonyms

My wife paints stones to give to her friends.

She collects them from the beach
small stones
bleached white by the sun
rubbed smooth by water and sand
she assigns each stone a word

hope
health
healing
grace
vision
joy

then glosses them with clear.

Etched in stone
takes a new meaning
the child of a friend
re-gave *listen* to her dad.

If I were to choose a stone
it would be *metaphor*.

Caprice

wind
this day
tart northwest
and bright
small crescendos
off and on
the bay
a virtuoso's
bow
dancing
down
strings
a squawking
glissando
sunshine
on water
pizzicato

Floating

July skies are peerless blue
bluer still floating off shore
body immersed in the bay
legs and arms splayed wide
head flat back for buoyancy.

Swans in flight or a stuttering cloud
either one releases the mind
current carries me down the beach
on my back without a thought
to put down my feet to swim ashore.

Still Light

Blood red
in quick ascent
the moon intrudes
secant by secant
on the eastern view
until it looms
over Silver Beach.
It dominates the sky
it decimates the night
it inundates the eye.
Caught off guard
stunned and outshone
the darkling bay below
bobs and weaves
still light on its feet.

Windfall

Prevailing winds from the southwest
have taken their toll on a black pine tree
the last one left standing
between my house and the bay.
Its spine distorted now
is aslant to the middle
then swept back in a bow
like the neck of a swan —
I am impressed by the power of wind
but I am touched by the beauty in bending.

A Sunset Sail with You

Down-wind
in a southerly breeze
yellow brick road to the setting sun
past Paradise Point to Peconic Bay
abeam of the buoy at Jessup's Neck.

Little fish fly
in a cascade glim
luminous on the leeward side
wind beats on the drum of the sail
water warbles along the chine.

Our wake flickers
like fireflies
a lucent phosphorescent curl
rounding the buoy at Nassau Point
a steeple in Cutchogue blesses the bay.

Crescent Beach at Robins Island
provides us shelter for anchorage
while a single gull in bas relief
keeps watch as we batten down
for the night.

Cartography

You are the seven seas ~

would that I were a fleet of ships
plying your surfaces
plumbing your depths
plotting your latitudes.

Vow at Summer's End

Somewhere sometime
in heaven on earth
we will be as one
two spirits on a single wing
soaring together in an azure sky
streaked with white wisps of cirrus.

We will grow in the woodland
our trunks entwined
and twisted like wisteria.

Swingtime

Dark hair pale skin bright eyes
gone this morning from the orchard swing
where only last night barely clad
in a shift of lightness
translucent in moonwhite
you swung out of summer.

Now only longing arcs through my mind
and the lisp of the bay whispers your name.

Now They Grow Roses

It takes fortitude patience and time to grow roses.

Because she is a romantic
she chooses roses with passionate names
and intriguing histories
Great Maiden's Blush Thigh of Nymph
Rose de la Paix.

Because he is a stay-at-home
he chooses roses from distant places
Italy China and France
Variegata di Bologna Chinensis Mutabilis
Comtesse du Cayla.

Because they are retired
and their children are grown
now they grow roses
Autumn Damask Twilight Mist
New Dawn.

Speaking of Fish

God made manifest in flesh
the flesh of fish.

I never heard a fish talk
but I did hear one sing
just offshore at Cedar Beach.
Never outside of the aquarium
had I seen such a fish
a fish of paradise with gossamer fins.
When it sang like a finch
high and sweet
I took the hook from its lip
and slipped it back in the bay
to return to that school
where it had mastered such scales.

Now I read that two men
heard a fish talk
a carp on its way to gefilte fish
Account for yourselves the end is near
are the words the fish said.
Some people claim that a righteous soul
can be reincarnated as a fish
the claim is met with disbelief
skepticism at the very best
but having heard a fish sing

I keep an open mind.

A Week on the Bay

Relieved of my work and earning a living
I am happy to vacation on Hog's Neck Bay.
My neighbors are farmers and baymen
who have no objection to sharing
their fields bays and backwaters.

I fish in the morning for weakfish and fluke
in the evening I listen to the muttering waves.
I go about my business each day
glad to be for the most part alone
except for the sun and the laughing gulls.

Fisherman's Beach

Summer has come and gone,
cars stream off the point
in a steady parade
packed with children, souvenir shells,
baskets of fresh picked tomatoes,
lucky found driftwood.
The day is overcast,
weather uncertain,
which makes it easy to get a jump
on Labor Day traffic.

Frothy concerns of July and August
are put away in suitcases
with cartooned beach towels
and half-squeezed tubes of Coppertone
where they will wait complacently
for another year to unfold itself.
The beach goes unnoticed now
except for old man Rowe
who scours the sand for sea worn glass
with his hands behind his back —

he is past seasons anyway.

Divine Rites

The sky is in tatters
black orange and white
with stained-glass drifters
migrant rulers of early autumn
on their wind-frayed way
to some ancestral grove
some monarchy in Mexico.

Wing-weary they stay their flight
silently gathering strength
on the nodding heads of blue hydrangeas.
How far will this respite take them
on their ragged flight home,
what compass keeps such beauty in line,
how great is the sum
of so many bright wings ?

North Fork Fall

It is fall now on the North Fork
and there is a certain conflagration
The flame has rekindled timid at first
just in the leaf of the maple tree
then on to the locust and oak
and every other canopy
In the warm and burnished light
of this October afternoon
it shows its colors tree by tree
until the countryside ignites
and every shoreline glows
with tawny russet-reds and gold.

You see it and you know
that fruition is at hand
you have lived another year
and with the grace of God
will live for many more
but now it's time to tend
to undone tasks and keep
the promises you've put on hold
and yes to make amends
In this bronzed and beryl place
after looking at His fire in the leaves
there is nothing left for which to ask

but spring.

Reflection

a bright spot
this morning
light on the bay

breasts quite white
a splash of mirth

a frothy
commotion
on sterling

the mirror bay
without wind

in itself
a marvelous
rarity

such fun
these loons

Equinox

Time
caught on its toe
like a ballerina mid-stage
just before her pirouette
equally poised
between night and day
between summer and fall
complete replete fulfilled
nothing left undone
nothing more to do
except to inhale
and fill these lungs
with the slap-dash amazement
of being alive.

Rose's Grove

I drift for bluefish
where the bay narrows
Robins island to the north
the wood pile to the south.
It is early November indian summer,
leaves have turned but trees are not bare,
terra-cotta auburn bronze,
wherever I look the colors of fall
console the bay.

East of the race
the sky has darkened.
I look intently for other signs
a change in wind increasing seas
but out of the east a long drawn vee
inscribes itself across the blue
a wedge of mallards overhead
from Shelter Island to Rose's Grove.

All afternoon as I fish
mallards cross-stitch the sky,
they navigate from bluff to bluff
homing on reflected light
sunlight from the sand bright bluffs
that line the bay on either side.
When I put in to port
although the fishing has been poor
I am exhilarated.

Perfection

A day like today
November 1
north from the bay
in the woodland at Laurel
that's where the trees
are tall and bare-legged
with tops of burnt orange
and antique gold
rich dark and deep
unspeakably autumn

It is just after noon
with barely a breeze
the sky is sharp-blue
the air crisp and clean
light is somnolent
whatever it touches
is burnished and buffed
brightness like a cat
climbs to high branches
preens there and purrs

Splashed by waves
sunshine and shade
wind thinned woods
are dappled and bright
alive with light
tree trunks washed
with blacks and grays
tree crowns aflame
The palette of fall
takes precedence here

The year has stopped
to catch its breath
you can hear one leaf
as it falls to earth
shadows are long
and well defined
seed has flourished
and ripened to fruit
April's brash promise
is kept by November.

Catching Sundown

By Thanksgiving
the sun has gone south,
it sets early now over Nassau Point.
A solitary man
can not get his arms around
so much beauty splashing down.
I step out on my deck
and, at the risk of being swept away,
immerse myself in overglow.
If I could catch
this incandesence streaming by
it might be light enough
to tide me over to another spring.

Snowbound

The bluffs at Jessup's Neck
are knee deep in snow
the woods on Cedar Beach Point
all crystal now
the trees are bent
in a graceful bow
to winter's prowess.
The race that separates
the point from the bluff
rarely subdued
is overpowered this day
by a bulwark of ice
set adrift by the tidal flow.

The sweeping view
of a blizzard on the bay
makes you catch your breath
and brings a welcome
slowness to our lives.
There's nothing else to do
but build a fire
uncork a jug of *North Fork Red*
and pray the power doesn't fail.
As winking night comes on
we're snowbound here
the two of us and Love
in winter's timeless trance.

Leit Motif

Fool's gold moon
overflowing the sky
grown too big for eyes
more than the heart can hold.
A mesmerist's charm
drawing the soul
up like water
crooning soft-shine
down like a rime.
Teetering on tall topped trees
tottering on slated roofs
toppling into the skater's pond
cracked light in shivers
adagio on ice.

SnowFly

Blue bird
on the sill
head cocked
beak to pane
looking for the one
who rain or shine
used to pour seed
and almost every day
kept the feeder filled.
No need to fly south
one can stand cold
if love is there
like food.

Duck Tips

There are two kinds of ducks
tippers and divers.
A mallard is a tipping duck
when it feeds
its bill goes down its tail goes up.
A bufflehead is a diving duck
it feeds under water
you never know where
it will bob back up.

Buffleheads appear in October.
The males are black and white
like little head waiters.
They hang out in a group,
when the first one dives
the others follow
except for a single stay-behind
who seems to stand guard.

I paddle my kayak into their midst.
The fat little ducks try to flee
but it takes them forever
to get off water into the air.
They will stay through winter
exuding charm and comic relief
even when the skies are gray
and the sun sets before supper time.

Cloud Nine

This is a house of cedar and light
that lives on water
and breathes salt air
that hears the wind
and watches the sky

It stands by the side of the bay
eye to eye with God
as silent as a fish
and as silver
as still as a heron
and blue.

Orient Blue

You have boarded the ship
about to set sail
then turn to find my face.
Our eyes do not meet
the glare from the glossy sea
is too great —
but not as great as my regret
seeing you go.

You have been at sea too long
seasons pass one by one
each morning I climb
the rooftop walk
to look through the glass
for some sign of a ship
your ship under full sail
but the horizon is bleak.
I turn my back to the sea
and think of us hand in hand
strolling through narrow lanes
that lead to the eastern bluffs
where we said our goodbyes.

Light from the albino moon
keeps me from sleeping
the firmament aglow before dawn
the disconsolate keen of mourning doves
the morning song of whippoorwills
each day more desolate and numb
with the realization you are not
you really are not
coming home.

Dwelling In Cedars

Robins Island is posted
I go there by boat and swim to shore.
You have to be willing to cross a line
because the island is patrolled
but once on the beach
you can slip through dunes
up the embankment
quite alone into quiet woods.

The tall trees are cedars
with bough-bare trunks
rising like pillars
twice a man's measure
to the lowest branches.
Beaded with sun
like drops of rain
the room below is dimly lit,
stillness stirs there
silence sounds
and the shade is infused
with the fragrance of cedars.

When dwelling under boughs
time is not at play,
I could stay the afternoon
adrift in Mr. Bacon's woods
but I have poached enough
Since wind and I have changed
it's time now to go home
light with the spirit of cedars.

Tacking Towards Home

My craft's a diminutive bark
that sails on a demitasse sea
thought is its rudder
whim is its wind
its wake is a ripple of me.

Acknowledgements

I am grateful to the editors of the publications where some of these poems first appeared:

        Avocet
        Maryknoll Magazine
        The Adirondack Review
        The Suffolk Times

I am especially grateful to Pat Swenson, the editor of Avocet, for her encouragement and support.

About the Author

Peter C. Leverich has been writing poetry for forty years. He attended Colgate University and the University of Missouri. He is the now retired founder and CEO of a computer software company.

The Performance Poets Association of Long Island recently awarded him first prize for his poem *Last Watch*.

He and his wife, Diane, live on the Peconic Bay in Southold, NY.